Nothin

Experiencing Fear and Vulnerability in Daily Life

Mary Booker

Published by:
Triarchy Press
Axminster, England

info@triarchypress.net
www.triarchypress.net

A catalogue record for this book is available from the British Library.

Print ISBN: 978-1-909470-80-4
ePub ISBN: 978-1-909470-81-1

For my mother

Contents

Acknowledgements

So many people have been part of the creation of this book. I would especially like to acknowledge:

Sandra for her insight, skill and compassion;

Andrew for his care and his enthusiasm for all things sensuous;

Caroline and Nik for seeing me, and for being there and listening;

all members of the *Move Into Life* Project Groups 1 & 2;

my daughter, Alice, for her love and permission;

Molly for teaching me the hardest of lessons;

and my husband, Chris, for hanging on in there and being my lover and best friend.

Nothing Special

I enter the sacred space,
carrying my uncertainty
and expectation.
"What do I need to do?"

Across the fire,
her eyes crease with
humour and a fierce kindness.
"Nothing special."

Introduction

However much we may wish not to think of it, and try to avoid feeling it, each of us is inescapably vulnerable. We are all subject to loneliness, loss, pain, grief and death. With life spans increasing, more and more of us will experience the ever-advancing decrepitude of old age. No matter how we try to shape it to our desires, our world is in constant flux. Along with all we know and love, we are temporary.

I chose to spend three years engaged in a creative project exploring fear and vulnerability. The initial challenges were to increase my awareness and tolerance of my own fear, become more embodied within fear and then work with it creatively. I discovered that, not only could I get better at all of these, but by doing so I was transforming my experience of being alive.

I did not have to seek fear out. By becoming more conscious of it, I discovered it is always there, part of daily experience. Fear became a gateway into vulnerability and vulnerability has led me into a deeper experience of connection with myself, with others and with the world around me. This is an ongoing process.

In opening to the aching, trembling vulnerability that is intrinsic to existence, I increasingly experience moments of intense joy and gratitude for my own being and the diverse, fragile, fleeting world I find myself a part of. Certainly, some things endure far longer than I will be able to. But even the rocks and the trees are ever-changing.

I know this experience is nothing special. It is always available – to everyone. But it has taken me a long time to open my shell enough to let it in on a regular basis. The poems in this book are about that opening. Vulnerability is vulnerable – and needs to be taken care of. Writing poetry and taking photographs are ways I can open to and care for my experience of vulnerability.

The poems here are organised in three parts:

Part One looks back into my childhood, especially at my mother, a woman who struggled to care for her own vulnerability, thus deeply affecting my journey with it.

Part Two contains four poems that arose from my exploration of fear and working creatively with it.

Part Three contains a variety of poems that express ways I am embracing and caring for the experience of vulnerability in my life now.

PART ONE

Looking Back

The Past

From the warmth of my mother's womb, I was pulled into a cold, clinical place. I was then swaddled and taken a long way away from my mother. I was kept alive by being placed in my mother's arms every four hours for 'ten minutes a side' and then taken away – to that other place – to be alone again. In 1949 that was what was happening in hospitals in the United States. The hospitalisation of birth was still in its early phase and overly confident of the benefits. Despite having had two previous successful home births in England, my mother found she had to argue and negotiate to be 'allowed' to breastfeed, but she did not feel able to fight the system any further.

For circumstantial reasons, this went on for two weeks – long enough for me to make some lasting accommodations to the conditions I had found myself in. My mother told me she breastfed me on demand once she finally got home – but she was already suffering post-natal depression, and I had become what she described as "a very good baby". My mother and I spent the rest of her life trying to find each other – and we never really did, despite both of us wanting it. By the time I had sufficient embodied wisdom to begin to create ways to connect with her, she was disappearing into Alzheimer's.

As a child I was solitary and described as "dreamy". My safe place was alone – and the wonderful natural landscape around our home in rural up-state New York provided a means of feeling connected to something, even if only through my imagination. Dream supplanted reality. Other people meant reality and were scary. But, the longing for close connection with another person never left me. Here, I look back and try to connect with both mother and child – vulnerable in their isolation.

Snow

She wanted to lie down.
It was not the reflection
of the house lights
sparkling on snow
that had drawn her out
into the night –
but the expanse of soft luminosity beyond –
framed by the long grey picket fence
and the dark cloaked sky.

In the still air
she felt an urge to scream –
to shatter the silence of snow.
Then, like a spell,
silence wrapped around her.
Snow welcomed her.

She had felt its call while
sitting in front of the fire,
darning a hole in another sock.
Suddenly the room was too warm –
the smell of pine suffocating.
Into the snow she went – and now
she wanted to lie down.

A few lingering flakes fell onto
her hot cheeks and melted.
She heard the baby crying –
and went inside.

Song to Myself, Aged 10

Here in the sun's first shining,
While all the rest are sleeping,
You can feel safe.
You can feel free –
a spirit unfurled,
waiting to be.
Dance in the night – and the storm.
You're not alone.

Let your eyes open to light –
eager and tender clear sight.
Lay on the grass.
Lean on the trees.
Breathe in the wind.
Move with the leaves.
Dance in the night – and the storm.
You're not alone.

Keep from the lies they will tell.
Hold to the dreams you can feel.
Know that you have
a taste for the truth.
Know that you are
love's living proof.
Dance in the night – and the storm.
You're not alone.

Dance in the night – and the storm.
You're not alone.

The Barn – Caroline, New York

Hovering for a while between fear
and the need to look inside,
I brace my feet and pull towards me
one half of the huge warped wooden door.
It takes all of my slight child weight
to slide it along the rusty rail,
revealing a gap big enough to squeeze through.

Sunlight enters unwelcome into the thick dusty darkness,
followed by my shadow.
Beyond is a great grey space –
smelt and felt rather than seen –
musty straw harvested before I was born,
bird droppings
and silence.

Turning, I look back at the sun-filled field,
crows scattering above it.
Behind me the darkness moves.
The air above me quivers.
Only when it has gone,
leaving as I had entered,
do I realise – owl!

Fresh

She stood at the kitchen sink with water
splashing over her hands – age spots and
so-fresh, golden yellow crook-necked squash.
Carefully picked-through green lima beans,
slipped from their furry pods, are
waiting on the so-stainless draining board.
Sweet corn cobs, still sheathed in their green and silk,
ready piled, on the window sill.
Fresh and sweet is best and only this is good enough.

She knew just how her sauce – nutmeg and black pepper –
would slide, shiny white, from the double boiler to
coat the freshly steamed vegetables, sprinkled with
chopped parsley from outside the back door.
Would it be good enough?

It was forty years since the girl –
tall and laughing –
slipped easily from the boulder into the icy Sierra stream –
water sliding down her face and body as she emerged –
fresh and triumphant –
onto the rocks on the other side.

Cake

Mable was the cleaning lady.
We thought of her as another mother,
more solid somehow than our own mother,
with arms and hands that could keep the world upright
the way it belonged.

She took us to her church suppers sometimes –
mashed potato, gravy and fried chicken –
nothing like we had at home –
so satisfying we went warm
and sleepy after.

Once our father took us
to the Fireman's Fair.
I won a cake, then discovered
that Mable had baked it –
thick, buttery pink frosting over
egg yolk yellow cake – two layers of it.
I still keep looking for another mouthful
of Mable's cake.

She was thinner the last time I saw her.
Someone took a photo of us together
outside the church in Slaterville.
I don't remember who.
I never went back.

Water, water, everywhere

Water, water, every where,
Nor any drop to drink.
my father recited with enthusiasm
as – aged four –
I leaned over the ship's rail
to take in
the great, grey Atlantic.

Water, water, everywhere…
I mused – aged forty –
at the end of a long pier,
watching his ashes
sinking beneath
the great, green Pacific.

(Samuel Taylor Coleridge, *The Rime of the Ancient Mariner*)

My Mother's Kitchen

My mother's kitchen was her kingdom.
She ruled there as despot and sage –
copper bottomed saucepans rubbed to a shine
with vinegar and salt –
cupboards with Lazy Susan circular trays
that turned around bringing
spices from China and India,
condiments from Italy and Japan,
spinning around into her easy reach.

Dishes were rinsed from right to left
and into the dishwasher –
but not the lead crystal
or the bone-handled knives.

She cooked with concentration,
subtlety and sincerity.
It was her poetry
and her pride.

But she was left walking through it
one heavy autumn day
with a spoon in her hand.
Looking at it, she turned to me and asked,
"What is this for?"

Gap Year

She turns her face to me – excited, unsure –
thick glass a barrier between traveller and
left-behind, holding-the-home heart.

I still feel her good-bye, I-love-you arms around me,
the scent of her hair all over my face –
the scent of her infant head
and the scant weight of her tiny body,
lying in my arms that first long sleep-not night.

Then I see my own mother's face –
full of pride and loss –
as I look down through the too-small window of the
plane
at her on the tarmac below –
good-bye hand raised.

My daughter's tears disappear into
Departures.

PART TWO

Working Creatively with Fear

The Fear Project

The *Working Creatively with Fear* project was born from a coming together of need and opportunity. My need to understand fear had been growing over many years. I am a dramatherapist and also train dramatherapists. I am comfortable embodying and holding difficult emotions like anger, pain and grief – my own and others – and I can open to and express empathy and love. But fear had been elusive. I had investigated different ways of working with fear, both through catharsis and through metaphor. Still it felt like I was not really going into it in any deep way. Both in the therapy space and the training space, I felt fear was not being addressed in the way that other emotions were. Clients and students would shy away from it. The fear of fear was powerful and difficult to move beyond – and I did not know how to help them with it.

When strong fear arose in myself, I experienced numbness and a kind of buzzing in the ears. In trying to explore it, I felt myself come to an invisible wall of some kind. Beyond this barrier the world lay, but I could not get to it. I recognised this as a familiar experience, reaching right back into childhood as far as I could remember. No effort on my part removed the barrier. I would just have to wait until the feeling passed – and, even then, a sense of isolation remained and at times this has taken me into depression. I know now that what I experienced was dissociation, and while it was just 'ordinary' dissociation, rather than the result of severe abuse or trauma, it had profound consequences for how I experienced life. I was over sixty now, and the need for greater connection was pressing hard. Fear was in my way.

The opportunity arose when dance movement psychotherapist, Sandra Reeve, offered a 'Project Group' where individuals could each investigate a personal project though the medium of movement. As soon as she invited me to join, I knew I wanted to investigate fear – give it my full attention – and see if I could finally understand how to move with and beyond it. I had worked with Sandra over a number of years and felt she could hold my process and support embodied understanding. Her *Move Into Life* approach, deeply informed by the *Joged Amerta* movement teachings of Suprapto Suryodarma, and grounded in the natural environment, seemed to reach out to the child glimpsed in the poems in Part One. The *Working Creatively with Fear* Project was born.

I was enthusiastic – ready to work with fear – and it did not disappoint me. Given permission to be there, fear arose quickly and persistently. With the support of Sandra and the Project Group, I had the time and conditions to feel fear in an embodied way, express it and reflect on my experience. I allowed myself to be curious about fear and read all the literature I could on its purpose, nature, meaning and consequences. This covered neurobiology, psychology, various therapy approaches and philosophy. My background in Buddhist meditation helped me become increasingly detailed in my observations of the visceral and mental processes of my own fear, now that it had been invited out to play. These combined contexts prevented me from becoming overwhelmed by fear and allowed me to develop a way to express it creatively. The creative product, or crystallisation, of my project was a performance of poems I wrote based on the fear experienced by some of Shakespeare's characters from *The Tempest.*

The Tempest arose as an idea early on in the project. It is my favourite Shakespeare play, and I had recently seen Footsbarn Theatre Company's *Indian Storm*, their 2012 version of *The Tempest.* Although I was not fully aware what it was saying to me, I was captivated again by the island (the place) and by Ariel and Caliban. Yet again, I felt angry with Prospero for treating people as objects he could manipulate. But this time, I was also aware of fear in the play – how it was affecting and motivating the characters.

Later on, I saw a performance of Thomas Adès's opera, *The Tempest*, at New York's Metropolitan Opera, courtesy of my local cinema. The singing brought the emotional themes to the fore. I was struck by the complex play of emotions in Prospero which he tries to suppress – his constant ambivalence and his fear of loss – and by the terror experienced by those on board the ship in the storm. Both of these I fed into the poems here, and the performance I created around them.

I read and re-read the play several times, as well as creative off-shoots from it, like W.H. Auden's *The Mirror and The Sea*. I was determined not to mangle Shakespeare – to be true to the text as it is given, while engaging with it emotionally in a way that allowed me to explore both my own fear and that of the characters – to find a creative place where we all met. That place had to be the island and, like Auden, the timing I chose was just after the end of the play. All of the poems I created came from the actual given circumstances in Shakespeare's text – blended with my own experiences and creative explorations.

'Caliban's Dream' was created from my experiences of being oppressed in various ways, particularly as a woman, and also inspired by the multitude of oppressions faced by displaced and disempowered people throughout history and into the present day. I also drew on my inner animal emotions and sexuality – rooted in body, instinct and the senses. I placed him on the rock that he has been confined to – a place of oppression. I first found my way into Caliban while moving outdoors during a Project Group exploration around 'blurring the boundaries'. Sandra suggested I go into the character with the intention of passing through it – knowing that costume so well I could put it down. I realised that to blur the boundary between myself and this character required my body, senses and imagination to work together and carry me through into Caliban, who was 'not me'. In the 'not me', I found something I had not expected. When, as Caliban, I saw a dandelion in the field, I awoke to his capacity for delight – that basic capacity for sensual delight that I had often noticed in children and in the profoundly disabled and autistic people I have worked with – my own fundamental sensual delight. This was taken from Caliban by Prospero, and the rock he was placed on connected me to the anger of his oppression.

'Ariel's Dream' was informed by an early childhood experience of being accidently almost smothered by one of my siblings, and by the fear throughout my childhood of my father's unpredictable anger. I placed Ariel in the woods and meadows of the island – places of magic for me like the woods and fields of my childhood. I explored the experience of flight, both as a fear response and as an expression of embodied freedom. The first happened spontaneously in an early Project Group session. Someone moving at floor level grabbed my ankle. When I tried to pull away, she did not release me. Suddenly, I shook myself loose, moved rapidly across the space and almost flew up onto the stage at one end and hid behind a display of flowers. I stayed there for the rest of the session allowing my body to express what I was feeling, both aware that I was actually safe and also in a state of fearful hyper-alertness. I had been taken by surprise and gone straight into flight. I felt delicate, hypersensitive. Later, I made the connection with Ariel.

It was not until I went to Java during that summer to work with movement teacher and performing artist, Suprapto Suryodarmo (Prapto), that I finally began to explore flight as an expression of embodied freedom. Prapto said, "Many people like to be free, but they are afraid to be free. Try out flying. How to connect when flying? How the cloud or the wind can connect." In the 1980s, when I first began actively to find a way to connect more with my body,

I worked hard to ground myself. It felt essential both to embodiment and to any possibility of working creatively with fear, and I still believe this is true. So I was surprised when Prapto said to me, "You are over your fear of falling! Not to bring it back!" It had never occurred to me that I might be over-grounding myself. In observing my movement he said my arms could fly but the rest was anchored and not flying. He suggested I work with images: "start with the image of a hammock between earth and sky. Then with the image of a bird...then other images of flying dragon, flying lion, flying tiger! When placing the feet, feel the air under and on the feet. Lifting knees more. Feeling the bottom. Relax the arms and shoulders. They are wings. Relax the neck. Allow it to move too." He also said that to learn to fly I needed to "start with safety" and that "even birds need to stop in a tree, on a rock". In other words, my grounding had its place. Prapto helped me begin to touch into a possibility of safety and connection coming from something within my body that he called a relaxed, empty axis. This allows a softer, lighter sense of being in my body and moving in the environment. To move as Ariel would be to "fly" from this embodied place.

I chose to write 'Ferdinand's Dream' because of the immensity of his fear (*With hair up-staring – then like reeds not hair*) and his loss (*His arms in this sad knot... something stained With grief*) – the way he seems to really feel them – and because, unlike others in the play, he is able to move beyond his fear and loss to love. For me, he is the one who, in the presence of trauma, really opens his heart and changes.

The final poem, 'Prospero's Awake', was not originally a part of the performance. After that first performance, during some 'movement for digestion' in the final Project Group session, I suddenly realised that, not only had I avoided dealing with Prospero, but he and I were profoundly connected through our shared tendency to revert to control as a defence against fear and vulnerability. I felt both anger and shame at this realisation. In the creative projection of character role – the 'not me' – I had avoided looking at my own shadow self. It took most of the following year for me to be able to write that final poem and add it to the performance which, therefore, needed to be done again. I was helped in this by seeing Roger Allam's performance of Prospero at London's Old Globe (also courtesy of my local cinema) which enabled me to see a much more human, tender side to this patriarch – and by support from the poet Alice Oswald, and her partner, poet and playwright Peter Oswald, who knew the play well. Peter reassured me that it was actually very difficult to get inside Prospero – he is a magician after all. During a four day creative writing residential with them at Sharpham House in Devon, I found the metaphor that allowed me to connect with Prospero – that of a gardener. I sweated out the poem in seven solid hours in the garden there, under an old tree overlooking the river. In Shakespeare's play, it is said about Prospero that *'tis a custom with him I' th' afternoon to sleep.* I imagined him as unable to sleep at night, because it had been at night that his brother had overcome him and usurped his dukedom. I placed him on a high cliff where he had a commanding view of the island and the sea.

PTSD – Post Tempest Survival Dreams

Centred on four characters in Shakespeare's play, *The Tempest*, these poems were woven together into a performance piece. There is much trauma within the play's narrative: betrayal, imprisonment, coercion, shipwreck, displacement and loss. I was interested in understanding and expressing the way in which each of these characters deals with the fear in their lives.

The setting is a small island hidden somewhere in the Mediterranean, controlled by Prospero, the deposed Duke of Milan, who practises magic. He lives in a cave with his daughter, Miranda. When the pair were first cast out to sea and ended up on the island, she was not yet three years old, but is now a young woman. In the play, twelve years on, his deposers sail near to the island by chance. Prospero enacts revenge on them by magically creating a storm and wrecking the ship. Finally, he reconciles with them, forgiving even his brother who had betrayed him. We arrive in the middle of the night after the end of the play. The three dreamers we will be visiting are:

- Caliban who is described by Shakespeare as *a savage and deformed slave*. He was discovered on the island by Prospero when he first arrived. His mother was a witch, Sycorax, who had died before Prospero came. Caliban was initially *made much of* by Prospero, who allowed Miranda to teach him language in return for Caliban showing him *all the qualities o' th' isle*. But as Miranda matured, Caliban lusted after her, and then Prospero enslaved him in a rocky part of the island. Prospero controls Caliban through his magic powers by sending him all manner of pain at night - *cramps, side-stitches, pinches, stings, aches...* Caliban feels he has been robbed of his inheritance.

- Ariel is described by Shakespeare as *an airy spirit.* Sycorax had imprisoned him within a pine tree because he *wast a spirit too delicate to act her earthly and abhorred commands.* Prospero had heard his moans and cries when he first came to the island. He used his own magic to free him, but then insisted Ariel obey his commands. Prospero always promised Ariel his freedom and finally releases him at the end of the play.

- Ferdinand is son to the King of Naples. His father was involved in deposing Prospero when Ferdinand was still a child. On Prospero's orders, Ariel created a storm that wrecked the ship Ferdinand and his father (and others involved in Prospero's deposition) were sailing in. All were in fact still alive, but Ferdinand was separated from them and believed them to be drowned. Ariel led Ferdinand to Prospero with sweet music, and he was first put to forced labour. He and Miranda fell in love, as Prospero hoped. He is promised her hand in marriage once they get back to Naples.

- Finally, we meet Prospero, who seldom sleeps at night, standing at his lookout over the sea.

The last phrase spoken by each character comes from Shakespeare's play.

Caliban's Dream

On my belly by the pool –
mushroom scent in my nostrils –
sweet singing in the trees above –
my hand slides under the cool, green water.
I wait for a fish to lie in my open palm,
mistaking it for sand or leaf to lay its eggs on.
I wait for the joyful springing of the trap –
the fleshy muscle squirming in my closed fist.
I drool in anticipation.

Throbbing in my groin!
My fist closes instead on my hard flesh.
The birds and breeze brushing through leaves
have become her voice – still high, still soft, still sweet.
And I smell her.
I smell her musky blood that calls up my own blood.
She is near.
Smell her! Must have her – now!
Seed must have earth!

Pain!
Like a knife cutting open my belly!
I curl to hold my insides inside.
The burden of endless bundles of wood
presses on my shoulders,
Sharp thorns cut deep into my skin.
I scream! I cry! No more!
Tears sting my eyes and burn down my face.
And I wake - on *this hard rock*.

Ariel's Dream

I cannot breathe!
Yet I have breath to scream – to groan – to howl!
Here is hell!
Hell is not fire – flames consume.
Hell is to never move.
I exist but cannot be me!
I was not made
to bear this torment.
Yet I cannot end it.

Air! – Light! – Space! – Breath!
My arms fly open and I lick the sunlight!
What is this?
I feel his will gently, relentlessly
wrap around my ankle,
pulling me, holding me.
Please! Master! Let me fly!
Pine tree's shadow is still there.
I must please him.

Now I fly!
The sun warmed sky opens to receive me.
Joy is mine!
No trace of human need or desire
taints my clear mind.
I laugh, spin and dance, dew soaked,
through the perfumed meadow.
Here I belong!
I drink the air before me!

Ferdinand's Dream

Over the deck and into the sea!
Water like castle walls falling down on me!
Then up to the surface like a barrel cork.
I hear screams of terror and echo them back,
only to have my mouth stuffed with brine.
Pushed under again into dark green places
unknown to me ever before – never again.
I am overtaken, overwhelmed, thrown about
with no more substance than feather, leaf or dust.
Lost! All is lost! I am lost!

My cheek presses on hard ground – wet sand
at the edge of the sea, the edge of the world.
All is calm, quiet, still –
but for a gentle rush of little waves over my feet.
I am nowhere I know – there is no one here.
There is nothing left of who I was
but the heart thumping in my chest.
I smell and taste the sea –
but hear now sweet sounds of heaven!

This harmony distracts me from my desolation.
And into my empty heart Beauty pours.
From sea and sand, past rock and shade and thicket,
Beauty's heart now leads me on.
I bless the exile that tore out my certainty.
Everything comes and goes.
Love has hold of my heart.
It *quickens what's dead and makes my labours pleasures.*

Prospero's Awake

I am tired –
overfull with the day's doings.
Sleep has always come hard
since that dark night's betrayal.
With all now seeming restored,
doubts like beetles alight and crawl.
It was I, turning inwards from my charge,
who allowed seeds of ambition to root in his heart –
where they still thrive.

A good gardener must make safe
his sweetest flower. Uprooted –
thrown onto a watery waste! I held her –
calmed her with stories, songs and prayers,
thus soothing my own terror and despair,
'til this island opened its kindly arms
and pulled us in.
Here was my charge – to create
a garden where a rose might bloom.

Nature's own magic I called forth,
bent to my purpose – now released.
Should I leave the rank and rampant weed,
cut back but not tamed,
to grow wild again?
Is a false, but forgiven, traitor safe?
I must make my uncertain way carefully –
weaker now. Yet, I am sure
This rough magic I here abjure.

PART THREE

Ordinary Vulnerability

Caring for Vulnerability

At the end of the performance of *PTSD – Post Tempest Survival Dreams*, I addressed this question to the audience: "How do you care for your own aching, inescapable vulnerability?" I then left the stage and sat in the audience, making it clear that it was a question for me to consider as well.

During the performance, as well as expressing my understanding of fear, I was aware of myself as vulnerable. I took care of my vulnerability by creating an aesthetic distance through fictional character roles, and by carefully crafting and rehearsing the performance. But to more deeply express my experience of vulnerability, I needed to find a more personal approach. In publicly sharing the poems in Parts One and Three of this book, I feel vulnerable.

Allowing and embracing vulnerability requires me to soften – to open to myself and to what is 'other'. It is a risk to relax defences – safety can only be relative. Feeling safe enough to soften is about developing sufficient contextual confidence over time, both in oneself and in the environment, to begin to tolerate being vulnerable and open to connection. Awareness, and an understanding of which contexts are safe enough to be vulnerable in and which are not, is necessary. I need to allow any habitual fear to arise without it overwhelming me or taking me into an old fear habit – assess the present context as safe enough – and then I need to soften.

One way I have noticed I can soften and open to my vulnerability is to become aware of my eyes – then soften my gaze, open my peripheral vision and sense the three dimensional space all around me. Somehow, I experience a connection between the eyes and the heart. Soft eyes bring soft heart – when looking at other people and also at the natural world. I feel vulnerable simply doing this. Once my eyes and heart soften, my whole body quickly softens too. As I soften, my other senses open as well and I begin to experience the world with a greater intensity – a relaxed intensity. Then sensory details emerge spontaneously and impress themselves upon me. From soft gaze and a sense of space around me and within me, I will suddenly be caught by some fine detail – this leaf, that glint in the other's eye, the touch of air on my skin.

I tend towards the natural world as a source of vulnerable connection. This was my childhood place of connection and it will probably always feel like the most reliable in which to be vulnerable. Many of the photos and poems that follow reflect this. They are about what is simple, often small and generally over-looked, rather than what is dramatic. These have always caught my photographer's eye – and are also what I love writing about. Natural, everyday, ordinary vulnerability is wonder-full, while being nothing special.

Last Year's Lessons (Imbolc)

Learning to:
Gather together the harvest.
Sort it. Store it.
Prepare it. Cook it.
Lay it on the table for others to taste, knowing
I won't be visiting those fields again.

Learning to:
Be still in the wakening.
Allow – nurture – refine the stillness.
Watch the earth move as it softens, releases and offers up
heart cracking beauty.
Mark and celebrate each new birth however small.
Experience gratitude as redemption.

Learning to:
Respect the limits in the loosening and the loss.
Ease but not heal the passing.
Witness the suffering – my own and others –
living and dying as best as we can,
falling into and out of relationship,
losing and sometimes finding each other.

The icicle hangs hard, cold, dripping,
as it passes from one reality to another
back to the flow.

Thorn Tree

Here I survive –
twisted and scarred –
sculpted by wind and ice –
rooted in rock –
comforted by sudden sunlight
and clear, clean air.
Where is home?

Brought here by bird
from mother hedge –
left to find my way
far from green lanes below.
Home is where I learn
to hold my ground and
let go to everything else.

There is joy in this.

Sacrament

Fixed and stretched between twigs
at the base of an old beech tree,
last autumn's web sparkles,
its pattern revealed in frost –
one corner undone, sticking to itself
and waving helplessly
as wind sweeps down the old track
from the moor.

The tree remains steady in the cold –
solid in a bank of earth and stone –
its sleeping heart still beating
deep down below
the hoary dead leaves.
Its only response to the wind
from the moor is to rake its fingers
across the night sky.

The sky is all moon tonight –
the distant stars overawed.
Haloed by ice,
wrapped in a luminous indigo cloak,
the moon is bright, benevolent, sublime –
a deity of light offering the blessing
of transfiguration
to moor, track, tree and web.

Recipe for a Walk to Kes Tor

From still and shaded lane
step with measured care
across bars of slippery steel.
Released onto open moor,
legs lap up the land.

Sheep shelter by ancient
remnants of huts and fields.
Wind lifts hair, blows
tedious ruminations
out into the distance.
Space opens up inside.

Scan dull, wind-flattened grass
for what the sun might catch
almost hidden within it –
blue stars of Milkwort,
yellow bundles of Birdsfoot,
tiny white Heath Bedstraw –
all open to the warmth
of the slowly setting sun.

Clouds shift to the horizon
and sunlight reflects off cars
on the distant Postbridge road.

Lay out face upwards
on the very top of
a primeval lava plug
that didn't quite surface
before it set hard.

The wind drops away.

Sit up and see that
tender light has crept up
on the grass below
and set it on fire.
No longer flat and dull,
it becomes the main show
set against the darkening blue
of the eastern sky where
a milk white half moon rises.

Memories of Blood

Blood –
wells up into a shining sphere
on the tip of the finger –
tastes metallic on the tongue –
floats in juices under the meat –
cakes the feathers of the dead bird –
drips from the nose onto the shirt –
hardens into a crust on the knee –
runs down the inside of the thigh –
floods from the gash on the forehead –
smears across the soft, tiny head –
slowly fills the hanging bag –
puddles on the floor –
throbs in the temple –
soaks through bandages –
rings in the ears –
races in the heart –
drains from the face.
Blood moves –
until it stops.

Grief is something we wear

I clothe myself in grief –
envelop my body
in grey-black voluminous stuff.
The wearer becomes the costume.
I am grief.

Gathering the fabric of it
carefully around myself,
I am bigger than before
and move slowly.
From inside this dark cloak
I look out at the not-grief,
the not-me, and feel safe
knowing what I am.

As I shuffle and turn,
a moan emerges from somewhere
inside the huge garment
and its wearer –
a sound that belongs to neither
and to both.

It becomes a howl.
The howl tears open grief,
shreds it,
and drops it to the ground.

Coney's Castle, Dorset

Some things touch the earth
so lightly
they barely seem there.

Tendrils of broken web
lace the scars
on a fallen branch.

Caught in them,
spent flowers from
the great beech overhead.

Lie down on the forest floor.
All around
is touching you.

Apricots

Fresh apricot is a soft pleasure.
Stroke with fingertips
 its skin – downy
 like a baby's –
or when ripe,
an old lady's –
gently wrinkled with
rouged cheeks.

Slight thumbnail pressure
and it splits into neat halves –
brown stone lying
in egg-yolk yellow flesh.

Altogether different when dried –
sweet, sticky,
pop-in-the-mouth perfect.

Heedless

One bush in the hedge trembles
as chittering sparrows
begin to roost.
In the blue shadows,
moths dip, flit and flutter,
drawn dangerously upwards
towards the still-warm tree tops
where swallows –
confident gypsies of the sky –
are dancing.

Coyotes

We all adapt to survive –
faces become masks,
hands slip into pockets,
legs cross,
chins dip.

Sentences trail off at the end –
excuse themselves.
Ideas slide back into
the darkness
before finding form.

Yet still we recognise
the song
when we hear it.
Like coyotes we –
sometimes –
howl for joy.

Skinny-dipping

There's only a few weeks of the year it's comfortable –
those warm water weeks
at the end of the summer.
And it's necessary to walk a good while,
then slide down steep paths
with stones rolling under your shoes –
or in a small boat seek out
inaccessible coves and strips of beach that
small children and couples with dogs
never reach.
Even then I keep near the cliff face
or hide behind large rocks.
A quick strip and dash –
no easing into the water –
straight in and over my shoulders.
Finally – cloaked in the sea –
my body opens and closes like a jelly fish –
received and receiving –
my skin one complete organ,
inside and out.
Why swim any other way?

Emergence

(*Breathe* – a sculpture by Tati Dennehy)

A long journey
prepared this moment.
Feet and hands
felt the way
through dark undergrowth –
frost-cracked stone –
gaps in rotting wood –
through seasons of searching
and touching
and leaving behind.
Naked and strong
I emerge to take
this breath.

Last Request

Let me not die
in a stuffy room.
Night or day,
let my last breath
be of fresh air
from a window
opened onto
a garden.

About the Author

Mary Booker was born in Ithaca, New York, of an English father and an American mother. She has been living in England since 1971, where she trained as a teacher and then as a dramatherapist.

Mary has practised dramatherapy with a wide range of client groups for almost thirty years, twenty-five of which she was also lecturer and trainer on the Devon-based MA in Dramatherapy. For eleven years she worked in special education as a multi-sensory impairment specialist, and wrote about this work in her book, *Developmental Drama: Dramatherapy Approaches for People with Profound or Severe Multiple Disabilities, Including Sensory Impairment* (Jessica Kingsley).

Mary lives in Exeter with her husband, Chris. Being close the sea and to her beloved Dartmoor, inspiration is on her doorstep.

About the Publisher

Triarchy Press is an independent publisher of interesting, original and alternative thinking (altThink) about:

- organisations and government, financial and social systems – and how to make them work better
- human beings and the ways in which they participate in the world – moving, walking, thinking, dreaming, suffering and loving.

www.triarchypress.net

Lightning Source UK Ltd.
Milton Keynes UK
UKIC01n2032210815
257348UK00012B/44